THE ... WHO PARDONED A TURKEY

And Other Wacky Tales of American History

ALLAN ZULLO

Illustrated by Arnie Ten

Watermill Press

To Frank Lang,
who knows so much about history—
because he's lived it for so long.

THE SILLY SIDE OF AMERICAN HISTORY

First off, American history is not boring! Sure, there are names and dates from a long time ago that you're supposed to know. But history is also full of riveting adventure, exciting drama, and incredible heroes and heroines. And oh, yes, American history also has goofs and gaffes, blunders and bloopers, and lots of funny stuff.

Let's begin with 1492, when Christopher Columbus sailed into the blue, landed in the Americas, and thought he was in India. Ever since, historians of our great nation have recorded one zany event after another.

This book describes some of the wacky but real people, places, and events that helped make our great country so . . . so . . . nutty! For example, you'll learn:

* Which president threw the wildest party ever in the White House.

* When celebrating Christmas was a crime in America.

* Why taking a bath could get you in trouble in colonial times.

* When Union and Confederate troops stopped in the middle of a Civil War battle—to chat and play cards.

This book presents the silly side of American history—the offbeat side that you probably won't find in any textbook.

Law and
Disorder

WHEN CHRISTMAS WAS A CRIME

Once upon a time, celebrating Christmas was a crime!

Back in the 1600s the Pilgrims outlawed all Yuletide celebrations. Lighting candles, singing carols, or eating a special holiday dinner could be done only behind locked doors. If you were caught, you could be fined or run out of town.

Even such simple joys as laughing, playing games, or merely resting on December 25 were severely frowned on by the Pilgrims.

Part of the reason for their strictness was that December was the month when the ancient Romans partied for seven days in honor of their god Saturn. The Pilgrims considered Christmas too serious an event to allow any connection with the Roman rites. The Pilgrims regarded Christmas as another day for hard work.

In 1659 the General Court (the legislature of the Massachusetts Bay Colony) passed a law declaring that anybody who was found observing Christmas by feasting, playing, or simply not working would be fined for every such offense.

The law banning Yuletide celebrations was eventually removed. Nevertheless, for nearly the next two centuries, Christmas remained a simple folk holiday with hardly any gift giving or religious observance. It wasn't until the mid-1800s that Christmas became one of the happiest, most festive, and most joyous times of year in the United States.

YOU'RE ARRESTED—FOR BEING LAZY

Other American colonies created their own tough laws.

In 1619, lawmakers in Jamestown, Virginia, passed sensible laws against gambling and drunkenness. But the legislators went a bit overboard by making it illegal to be lazy and to wear gaudy clothes. All colonists were also required to attend *two* church services every Sunday.

Among the crimes that colonists in Massachusetts faced punishment for in the 1650s were eavesdropping, scolding, neglect of work, failing to help a poor person in distress, smoking, playing cards, and pulling hair.

The Puritans believed that all "bawdy ballads"—and music in general—were "useless frivolity." Dancing, too, was a no-no, but many colonists tended to ignore that part of the law.

EVERYONE'S A CRITIC

An acting troupe in Providence, Rhode Island, nearly was beaten up in 1761 because the audience didn't like their performance.

A sour-faced mob who thought laughter was sinful nearly went crazy with rage after the David Douglass Histrionic Academy put on a comedy by William Shakespeare. Douglass tried to talk some sense into the angry crowd, but that only inflamed their fury.

The situation turned so ugly that a prominent citizen who supported the actors trained a cannon on the mob and threatened to open fire if the crowd didn't leave. They reluctantly left—and Douglass decided not to perform any more Shakespeare for a while.

KIDS ARRESTED FOR SLEDDING!

Some towns just didn't want kids to have fun in the wintertime.

Back in 1713, in Albany, New York, a law was passed that stated that "children . . . do very disorderly [things] to the shame and scandal of their parents" when they "ride down the hills in the streets . . . with small and great sleds . . . by which accidents may come." As a result it was declared "lawful for any policeman to take . . . and break any sled . . . in pieces."

THE STUBBORN CHILD LAW

Be thankful you didn't grow up in colonial times. Adults didn't take *any* lip from kids back then.

Believe it or not, a teen over the age of 16 who rebelled against his or her parents could be punished by *death*! It was called the "Stubborn Child Law." Kids who swore at their parents or refused to obey them were subject to this extremely harsh penalty.

Fortunately the death penalty was never actually carried out. Historians believe the law was commonly used as a threat against children who didn't behave.

JAILED—FOR LIVING ALONE!

You could be jailed in early America simply for living by yourself.

Far from being the land of the free, the New England colonies had laws controlling their citizens' every move.

Among the strangest of 17th-century laws:

• Living alone was a criminal offense—because some lawmakers thought there would be nobody around to prevent a person from sinning. When someone was caught living alone, the local judge would order the person to move in with a respectable family. A person who refused would be jailed until he or she had a change of mind.

• It was against the law for ordinary people to wear fancy clothes. Only rich people were legally permitted to put on pretty and expensive clothes made from silk or adorned with gold buttons. Everyone else was supposed to wear simple clothes made from cotton and wool.

• On Sundays most activities that did not involve religion were forbidden. That included traveling, chopping wood, cooking a meal, hoeing the garden—even kissing your parents!

CLEANLINESS IS *NOT* ALWAYS
NEXT TO GODLINESS

In the old days, taking baths could get you in hot water.

Many colonists believed that bathing led to sin. Laws in Virginia and Pennsylvania either limited bathing or banned it outright.

In Philadelphia anyone who bathed more than once a month actually faced jail!

AND THE BRIDE WORE A
STUNNING (NIGHT)GOWN

Today most brides get married in beautiful white wedding gowns. But back in colonial New England

many women wed in their nightgowns!

According to an old English tradition if a woman married "in her shift [a nightgown] on the king's highway," her husband would not be responsible for any debts she owed before her marriage. Colonists carried that tradition to the New World.

Getting married in your nightie was a bit embarrassing, so some of these weddings were held at night on a lonely road.

But of course other couples preferred to marry indoors during the day. One such couple who wed during the day avoided embarrassment by sticking the nightgown-clad bride in a closet with only her hand sticking out!

TOWNS SETTLE DISPUTE
WITH THEIR FISTS

The colonial Connecticut towns of Lyme and New London once had a dispute over a small piece of land claimed by both towns.

Officials knew it would take too much time, energy, and money to reach an agreement through the courts. So the towns found a "handy" way to resolve the matter—by putting up their dukes!

Lyme matched its two best fistfighters, whose last names were Ely and Griswold, against New London's top brawlers, Ricket and Latimer. The four met in a field and slugged it out with their fists. Griswold and Ely won, thereby giving Lyme undisputed ownership of the property.

MAN THROWN IN JAIL—
FOR WEARING A BEARD!

Joseph Palmer was tossed in jail—for wearing a beard!

Palmer, a 42-year-old farmer, moved his family to Fitchburg, Massachusetts, in 1830. He was a nice enough fellow. There was only one problem—he sported a long, Santa Claus-like beard. Today that's no big deal. But back then he was one of the very few men on the East Coast to wear a full beard.

The citizens of Fitchburg reminded Palmer that no great American—from George Washington to their current president, Andrew Jackson—had ever sported such whiskers. Palmer ignored his neighbors. So whenever he went for a walk, people jeered him. They even threw stones through the windows of his house.

One day four men—armed with scissors, soap, a shaving brush, and a razor—ambushed Palmer. They wrestled him to the ground and tried to shave off his whiskers! But Palmer fought back fiercely, and his attackers fled. Even though he was the one who had been assaulted, Palmer was arrested and thrown in jail! He was found guilty and ordered to pay a fine.

Palmer, a man of principle, refused to pay, so he remained in prison. Within a few months freedom-loving people throughout New England learned of his plight and rallied to his support, demanding his release.

After Palmer spent nearly a year in jail, weary officials told him he could go home. But he refused to go home unless they publicly admitted that he had every right to wear a beard. Not wanting to lose face, the officials refused. So Palmer stayed in his cell.

Eventually the jailers found a way to put an end to his—now their—ordeal. One day they picked up Palmer in a chair, carried him outside, and dumped him in the street.

WACKY LAWS ABOUT WOMEN

Believe it or not, it used to be illegal in Delaware for women to propose marriage in a leap year!

That's just one of the crazy laws against regulating women's behavior that were once on the books in the United States. Here are some other ones:

• In Kentucky a woman couldn't walk along a road in a bathing suit unless she was with at least two police officers—or armed with a club!

• In the same state, it was illegal for a woman to buy a hat unless her husband tried it on first.

• San Francisco women were prohibited by law from spraying their laundry by squirting water from their mouths.

• New York City prohibited women from smoking cigarettes in public places. One lady who broke the law in 1904 was actually thrown in jail.

• In some states an unescorted woman could be refused a meal at a restaurant or a room at a hotel.

• At the turn of the century a third of the states said that a woman had no legal claim to her own hard-earned money—even if she was working to support a lazy husband.

• Until 1882 a husband owned the clothing and jewelry that he gave to his wife.

MEN ARRESTED FOR SWIMMING TOPLESS!

In the late 1800s it was illegal for men to wear topless bathing suits in New York.

For years, when men went to the beach, they were expected to wear tank suits that went from the shoulders to the thighs. By the 1930s some men were getting fed up with these ridiculous suits and switched to swimming trunks. But swimming trunks were too shocking for most people—and against the law.

In 1934 eight men were fined a dollar each for topless swimming at New York's Coney Island beach. The woman judge told them, "There are many people who object to seeing so much of the human body exposed." A year later 42 men in swimming trunks were arrested in Atlantic City, New Jersey. An official there claimed, "We will have no gorillas on our beaches."

Fortunately, by the end of the 1930s, most laws against bare-chested men at the beach had been wiped out.

PRESIDENTS ARE PEOPLE, TOO

HIS HIGHNESS, GEORGE WASHINGTON

The first U.S. Senate had a problem. They didn't know what to call the president of our country. After all, the United States had never had a president before.

A committee was formed in 1789 to decide on the proper form of address for President George Washington. After three weeks of study the committee declared that Washington would be referred to as "His Highness, the President of the United States of America, and Protector of their Liberties." Luckily, the title didn't stick.

WASHINGTON WANTED TO JOIN THE BRITISH NAVY

The Father of Our Country once wanted to become a naval officer—in the British Royal Navy! Washington's half brother Lawrence had served as a captain in a British fleet that fought the Spanish off the South American coast. In 1746 Lawrence, who was 28, wrote to George, then 14 years old, about the exciting naval battles he had encountered. Lawrence told George there was an opening for a midshipman on a British naval ship then sailing in Virginia waters.

George wanted to join the British navy at once. But because he was underage, his mother, Mary Ball Washington, had to give her permission. Mary refused to let the teenager sign up—and thus steered him onto a course that ultimately made history.

PRESIDENT SPENDS MORNINGS SKINNY-DIPPING

Just because he was president of the United States was no reason why John Quincy Adams couldn't enjoy the fun of skinny-dipping.

In the 1820s the White House's front yard overlooked the Potomac River. That was perfect for President Adams. On summer mornings during his one four-year term, he liked to slip down to the river between 4 A.M. and 6 A.M. He would disrobe, leave his clothes piled neatly under a tree, and plunge into the river for a quick dip.

Early risers who walked along the river's edge often spotted the portly president, who was an excellent swimmer, enjoying his morning ritual. Coming out of the water, he would dry off and put on his clothes. Then he would stroll back to his study to read the Bible and the newspapers before his breakfast at 9 A.M.

Although many people knew about Adams' predawn skinny-dips, they usually left him alone. But in 1829 one female reporter named Anne Royall took full advantage of the president's nude swims. For days he had been ducking her attempts at an interview. So one morning, after Adams had taken off his clothes and jumped in the water, the woman reporter showed up. She then sat on his clothes. The modest and embarrassed Adams was forced to stay in the water until he agreed to grant her an exclusive interview (one during which he would be fully dressed!).

FAIR-WEATHER FRIENDS

In 1800, when John Adams was president, a new town in New Hampshire chose to name itself Adams in honor of the country's chief executive. The town was doubly pleased when Adams' son, John Quincy Adams, became our sixth president.

Nevertheless, when John Quincy Adams lost to Andrew Jackson in the 1828 election, the town turned on the Adams family. Adams, New Hampshire, changed its name to Jackson in 1829.

WHITE HOUSE TURNS INTO ANIMAL HOUSE!

Andrew Jackson was a decorated war hero, a man who never ducked a fight. He fought Native Americans, the British, and outlaws. Yet one of the scariest times in his life came not during a battle but from a wild party that got out of hand—in the White House!

When Jackson was elected president in 1828, he became the country's first commander in chief who did not come from a wealthy, well-connected family. Jackson was a man of the people.

After his inauguration, which was followed by a grand parade down Pennsylvania Avenue, Jackson threw open the doors of the White House for an evening reception for the general public. Although it was a fine gesture by the president, it turned into a disaster.

Following their idol, 20,000 Jackson supporters streamed into the White House. Without a care in the world the enthusiastic crowd, many in muddy boots, climbed over furniture, including expensive chairs, tables, and rugs. They carelessly broke thousands of dollars worth of china and crystal as they lunged for drinks.

At one point the party animals' wild night became too dangerous for the president to remain in the White House. In their joy, Jackson's out-of-control supporters wanted to pick him up on their shoulders and toss him around. Fearing for his safety, a group of levelheaded young men formed a line and locked arms, allowing the president to escape through a rear door.

Jackson never threw a party for the general public again.

PRESIDENT TALKS HIMSELF TO DEATH

The longest-ever inaugural address resulted in the shortest-ever presidency.

William Henry Harrison, the ninth president of the United States, insisted on delivering his inaugural speech outside on a freezing-cold day— and talked for a tongue-numbing hour and 45 minutes! No president before or since rambled on for such a long time.

Despite stormy, blustery weather the 68-year-old president refused to wear a coat or hat because he wanted to live up to his image as a tough war hero and frontier fighter.

Harrison's secretary of state, Daniel Webster, tried to talk him into delivering a shorter speech. But the president refused. On March 4, 1841, Harrison read his lengthy (8,578-word) address in the terrible weather. As a result Harrison caught an awful cold. Tragically it developed into pneumonia, and he died on April 4, 1841—just 31 days after giving his speech.

William Henry Harrison went down in history for serving the briefest official term as president.

Parties, Sleeps Through Term . . .

U.S. PRESIDENT LASTS ONE DAY IN OFFICE!

David Rice Atchison had the shortest term ever as president of the United States—one day!

Yet history books refuse to recognize Atchison as the nation's twelfth chief executive, even though, according to the Constitution, he legally was in charge of running the country for 24 hours.

As president, Atchison never stepped foot in the White House, nor did he sign any bills. In fact, he didn't do much of anything during his term except party and sleep.

Atchison, a Missouri senator, was president *pro tempore* of the Senate on March 4, 1849—the day President James K. Polk's term expired at noon. Zachary Taylor was scheduled to take over as president. But March 4 was a Sunday, and Taylor, a very religious man, refused to violate the Sabbath by taking the oath of office on a Sunday.

Because Polk's vice president, George M. Dallas, had resigned a few days earlier, Atchison was technically the only person legally allowed to exercise the powers of the presidency from noon

March 4 until noon March 5, 1849. Under the Succession Act of 1792 Atchison as president of the Senate was third in line for the presidency and thus automatically became president of the United States, because the presidency and vice presidency were vacant.

No president ever took his high office as lightly as Atchison did. First he appointed a number of his buddies to cabinet positions—with the understanding that they would do absolutely nothing during their one-day terms. Then he threw a party for them. Finally the 24-hour president excused himself, shuffled off to his bedroom, and slept out the remainder of his administration.

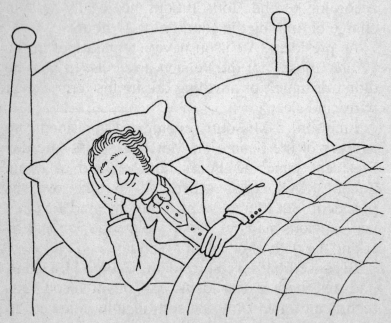

On Monday at noon Zachary Taylor took over as the country's chief executive, ending the most peaceful—and shortest—presidency in American history.

Speeds Through Town in Buggy . . .
PRESIDENT GRANT ARRESTED!

In 1875 President Ulysses S. Grant hopped into his horse-drawn buggy at the White House and took off at a high rate of speed through the streets of Washington, D.C.

At M Street, police officer William West spotted a horse and buggy driving west at a dangerous speed. As they sped toward him, Officer West seized the horse's bridle and was dragged half a block before he could stop the animal. Then West angrily walked up to the driver to arrest him—and realized the driver was none other than the President of the United States.

"I'm so sorry, Mr. President," gasped the stunned police officer. "I had no idea it was you."

Grant wasn't the kind of person to ask for any special favors. "Officer," the president ordered, "do your duty." So West arrested the president on the spot and, following the laws of the city at the time, took the horse, buggy, and driver to the police station. Grant, who posted a 20-dollar bond and was released, returned to the White House on foot. The speeding charge was never pressed. Grant later wrote a letter to West's superior commending West for doing his duty.

It wasn't the first time Grant had been caught speeding. By the time he took office in 1869, Grant already had received two speeding tickets and been fined five dollars for each offense.

A few years after he left the White House, Grant went on a fishing trip in Pennsylvania. To his surprise he learned that he was fishing out of season. Grant went to the nearest justice of the peace and turned himself in. At first the justice refused to fine the former president. After all, his was an honest mistake. But Grant insisted on paying the full fine and then scolded the justice for not being more zealous in enforcing the law.

President Fears Electricity . . .

DON'T TOUCH THAT SWITCH!

During Benjamin Harrison's term as President (1889-1893), electric lights were installed in the White House.

You would think that the First Family would be thrilled to have electrical power at the flick of a switch. But not the Harrisons. They were scared of electricity and feared that they could get electrocuted by turning on a light. So the First Family had the White House electrician flip the switches on and off for them.

SORRY TO INTERRUPT YOUR NAP, MR. PRESIDENT, BUT DO YOU PLAN TO WORK TODAY?

Calvin Coolidge may have been America's most

relaxed president.

Throughout his terms in office (1923-1929), Coolidge worked an average of only four or five hours a day.

On a typical day Coolidge would rise around 6 A.M. He took his time getting dressed and eating breakfast and rarely went into the Oval Office until after 9 A.M. He broke for lunch around noon and then took a two-hour nap. After another hour or two of work in the late afternoon, he would call it quits around 5 P.M.

The president often went to bed by 8 P.M. and snoozed for ten hours before starting his day all over again. One night, when Coolidge stunned local citizens by attending a play, comedian Groucho Marx joked, "Isn't it past your bedtime, Calvin?"

Coolidge spent more time on vacation than any other president before or after him. Each summer he would knock off work for a lengthy two or three months and relax in the countryside, where he liked to fish. Among his favorite places were the Black Hills of South Dakota; White Pine Camp, New York; and Swampscott, Massachusetts. He chose isolated spots because he didn't want to be bothered by government officials or even phone calls.

Having succeeded to the presidency on Warren Harding's death in 1923, Coolidge completed a full term on his own after being elected in 1924. He had the right to run for office again in 1928, but he declined. The rigors of the four-hour work day apparently were too much for him.

HAIL TO THE CHIEF PETS

Furred and feathered, horned and hoofed, presidential pets have occupied a favorite place in American history. Among the capital companions:

• Dick—Thomas Jefferson's pet mockingbird, who liked to follow him to bed each evening.

• Poll—Andrew Jackson's pet parrot, who often uttered impolite words.

• Whitey— Zachary Taylor's favorite horse, who had served Old Rough and Ready well during the Mexican War. Rather than keep the horse on a farm outside of town, Taylor insisted that Whitey remain with him. So the horse used the White House lawn as his private pasture.

- Pauline Wayne—William Taft's pet cow, who grazed on the White House lawn.
- Old Ike—Woodrow Wilson's ram, who liked to chew tobacco, especially cigar stubs.
- Rebecca—Calvin Coolidge's pet raccoon, who walked around the White House on a leash.
- Zsa Zsa—John F. Kennedy's pet rabbit.

Theodore Roosevelt kept a young lion and several bear cubs at the White House. William McKinley owned a Mexican yellow parrot and some roosters, much to the dismay of neighbors.

Although many First Families thought the squirrels who lived on the White House grounds were cute, President Dwight Eisenhower wasn't one of them. He loved golf and used to practice his putting on the White House lawn. When squirrels interfered with his golfing concentration, the frustrated president ordered their removal. The squirrels were humanely trapped and released miles away from the White House.

LINCOLN GRANTS PRESIDENTIAL PARDON—TO A TURKEY

During the Christmas holidays President Lincoln and the First Family were presented with a fat, live turkey as a gift.

Lincoln's eight-year-old son, Tad, quickly became attached to the gobbler, who followed him around the White House lawn. When Tad learned the turkey was about to be beheaded for a holiday

dinner, he burst into tears. He had to save the bird.

Tad pleaded his case to his father. Lincoln was so moved that he interrupted a cabinet meeting just to issue a presidential pardon for the lucky bird.

The Lincolns then kept the turkey as a pet and named him Jack.

DID YOU KNOW . . .

• George Washington seldom smiled because he was afraid of losing his dentures.

• The White House did not have indoor plumbing until 1833—33 years after it was opened.

• Andrew Jackson was the only president who did not believe the earth was round.

• Harry Truman was so down to earth that he always washed his own socks.

WAR AND PEACE

BATTLE OF TRENTON
LOST OVER CARD GAME

The colonists gained their first major victory of the Revolutionary War—the Battle of Trenton—because the enemy's commander did not want his card game disturbed!

In December 1776, German soldiers, known as Hessians, were fighting for England. They had built a fort at Trenton, New Jersey. George Washington and his desperate Continental Army forces huddled a few miles away.

The Hessians were led by Johann Rall, a colonel who hated Americans and totally underestimated them. He rejected pleas by some of his junior officers to increase protection around the town against Washington's rag-tag soldiers. "Let them come!" he declared. "We need no trenches. We'll go after them with the bayonet."

Rall was more concerned about his own comfort than the war. Headquartered at the house of a leading loyalist, the Hessian colonel demanded the best in clothes and food. He relaxed by playing cards for hours with his officers and prominent Tories, backers of the King of England.

In the days before Christmas, Rall's card games were often interrupted by reports from local citizens that the Americans were drawing rations for a march of several days—obviously part of a plan to attack Trenton.

Irritated by these "wild, baseless stories," Rall gave strict instructions not to be bothered by any more such reports—especially while he was playing cards.

On the day after Christmas a loyalist spy appeared outside Rall's headquarters with an urgent message. But the Hessian guards wouldn't let him enter because they did not want to disturb the colonel. So the spy told a junior officer that Washington and his men had secretly crossed the Delaware River that morning and were advancing on Trenton.

Despite this important news the junior officer—who had been scolded for interrupting Rall's card game the day before—refused to let the spy enter the Hessian headquarters. Instead he ordered the spy to write down his message. A porter then took the note into the house and timidly handed it to Rall.

Annoyed by the porter, the colonel refused to interrupt his card game and thrust the note, unread, into his pocket. By the time he had played his hand, Rall had completely forgotten about the message—one that could have changed the course of the Revolutionary War.

The colonel would soon regret his do-not-disturb orders. He was still playing cards when Washington and his army attacked Trenton. Without time to organize or rally, the entire Hessian army quickly was captured.

During the battle Colonel Rall was shot. As he lay dying, he swore that if he had read the loyalist's message, the revolutionaries never would have taken his army—or his life.

SO WHERE'S THE REST OF HIM?

One of America's strangest memorials to a war hero honors revolutionary soldier Benedict Arnold.

Arnold served bravely on the colonists' side at the beginning of the Revolutionary War. He was wounded in his left leg at the Battle of Saratoga in New York. Yet later, after he recovered, Arnold went over to the British side and became a traitor in the eyes of his former comrades-in-arms.

Years later the people in Saratoga wanted to erect a Revolutionary War monument. They wanted to pay respect to Arnold's bravery and the wounds he suffered while fighting for the colonists. On the other hand, the people didn't want to glorify a traitor.

The problem was solved by putting up a monument in Saratoga National Historical Park—to Arnold's left leg and nothing more! The monument shows a left boot and explains Arnold's achievements—but leaves out his name.

U.S. ARMY'S WEIRDEST UNIT—
THE CAMEL CORPS

The U.S. Army once recruited camels into its service.

In 1855 Congress voted to spend 30,000 dollars to buy camels to help settle the West. The camel requires about as much food and water as a horse, but it doesn't sweat or get as hot as a horse does. The camel eats almost anything and stores much of its food in its hump, which is plump when the animal is on a regular diet and nearly flat when the animal has gone days without food. The camel also can travel 300 miles in four days without a water break (as long as it drinks 30 gallons of water before the trip).

Major Henry Wayne and government official David Porter went to Africa and bought 33 camels.

They also hired several camel drivers who knew how to handle the beasts. The camels were then shipped to Indianola, Texas, in 1856. When the camels arrived, they were laughed at by townspeople, who doubted the animals' strength and usefulness. Major Wayne took this as a challenge.

In front of a large crowd he made a camel kneel and strapped over 1,200 pounds of cargo on its back. On the major's signal, the camel easily stood up and walked off. The crowd shouted praises for the funny-looking animal.

After a second shipment of camels arrived in 1857, bringing the total to 75, the 1st U.S. Army Camel Corps was formed.

Despite the advantages of camels over horses, most people had a low regard for the animals. To answer his

critics, Lieutenant Edward Beale, commander of the Camel Corps, used the beasts to open up a new supply route across the desert between New Mexico and California. The camels handled the rocky terrain, desert, and mountains with ease.

Along the way, however, the unfamiliar camels caused passing horses and mules to take fright and bolt. On seeing an approaching wagon, an advance man from the Camel Corps would ride his specially trained horse toward the wagon and shout, "The camels are coming! The camels are coming!"

Camels also carried mail between Army posts and small settlements in the old West. At the end of the first year of the Camel Corps, Lieutenant Beale told Congress, "I have tested the value of the camels, marked a new road to the Pacific, and traveled 4,000 miles without an accident." The secretary of war was so impressed that he asked for 1,000 more camels from the Middle East. But while Congress debated the request, the Civil War broke out. The Camel Corps was soon disbanded.

Of the original 75 camels, 28 were given to the city of Los Angeles, which used them to transport mail and cargo. The rest were auctioned off. Some ended up in a circus; others were put to work for a freight service.

Almost everyone forgot about the camels until one of the handlers felt slighted that he had not been invited to a picnic in Los Angeles. He broke up the gathering by roaring through it in a cart pulled by one of his beloved camels.

YOU DIDN'T DO YOUR LAUNDRY?
12 LASHES WITH THE WHIP!

Back in the 1800s a sailor in the U.S. Navy who didn't do his laundry or keep his mess kit clean could expect a painful punishment—getting lashed with a whip.

According to an 1848 Navy list of misdeeds and their consequences, a sailor would receive 12 strokes of the whip across his back for the following offenses:
- bad cooking
- stealing a major's wig
- using bad language
- wearing dirty and unwashed clothes
- neglecting to keep his mess kit clean

A sailor would receive six strokes of the whip for:
- being too noisy while on the ship
- throwing overboard the top of a spittoon
- running up and down a ship's rigging

I WILL NOT TELL A LIE

When the Civil War broke out, the Union Army wouldn't take teenage boys under the age of 18 even though many had volunteered.

Rather than walk into the recruiting office and lie outright, underage volunteers came up with a clever scheme. They would scribble the number 18 on a scrap of paper and place it in the sole of their shoe. Then, when an Army official would ask their age, the boys could truthfully reply, "I am over 18."

Fight or Surrender?

COLONEL ASKS FOR ADVICE—
FROM THE ENEMY

During the Civil War a Union commander crossed the battle lines to ask the enemy whether he should fight or surrender.

At the battle of Munfordville, Kentucky, in 1862, Colonel John Wilder found that he and his 4,000 men were surrounded and outnumbered six to one by Confederate forces. Wilder was not an experienced soldier. He had been an engineer and industrialist in Indiana before the war broke out. Since he lacked the knowledge and confidence to do the right thing as commander, he sought professional help—from the enemy.

Waving a white flag, Wilder entered the Confederates' camp and asked General Braxton Bragg what to do. Bragg refused to answer. Instead the rebel general invited Wilder to count the number of cannons trained on the Union forces. Wilder soon realized the rebels had enough artillery to demolish his position in a few hours. He didn't even finish counting all the cannons when he told Bragg, "I believe I'll surrender."

Opposing Soldiers Even Play Cards!

ENEMIES STOP IN MIDDLE OF BATTLE—
TO EXCHANGE GREETINGS

In one of the most bizarre battles fought in the Civil War, Union and Confederate troops occasionally called a truce and stopped fighting. Then they would meet halfway, exchange greetings,

trade goods, and even play cards. When they finished, they went back to their respective positions—and tried to kill each other!

It all happened in a cornfield in Petersburg, Virginia.

According to a newspaper account of the battle, the "opposing pickets . . . would, in spite of all, occasionally creep into a cornfield for a friendly chat, or for a barter, or for a game of cards!

"Two [opposing soldiers] were playing a game one day, with Abe Lincoln and [Confederate President] Jeff Davis as imaginary stakes. The [Union soldier] lost. 'There,' says the winner, 'Old Abe belongs to me.' 'Well, I'll send him over by the Petersburg express,' jokingly responded the defeated Yank.

"At another time, there had been lively shelling. After dinner there was a slackening of hostilities. A [rebel] rose up from his line and shook a white paper as a sign of truce, then sprang over into the cornfield. At once a hundred men from either line were side by side, swapping tobacco for coffee or jack-knives, hard tack or sugar for corn cake.

"New acquaintances were made. In some instances, old acquaintances were revived. A Connecticut officer found a kinsman in a rebel officer. One found a brother on the other side, and yet another his own father!

"After a little time, the swapping of the day was done, and officers and men returned to their respective lines. All was quiet again until the artillery reopened fire."

HE HAD A BURNING DESIRE TO MEET STONEWALL

During the height of the Civil War a Confederate soldier was brought before his commander for breaking the rules by twice burning fence rails at a rebel encampment. The soldier was then sent to General Stonewall Jackson—one of the South's most famous generals—for punishment.

When Jackson asked the soldier why he was burning the fence rails, the man replied, "I've been enlisted for eight months, and in all that time I never could get a good look at you. So I thought I would burn some fence rails. I knew then I would get sent to you."

Jackson then turned to the guard and said, "Take this man and set him on the top of that empty barrel in front of my tent. The front of my tent is open, and he can look at me as much as he likes."

For the next several hours the soldier quietly and

happily stood on the barrel and watched his war hero write letters inside his tent.

THOSE CLOTHES AREN'T FIT
FOR A PRESIDENT

When Confederate President Jefferson Davis was captured by Union troops in 1865, they were shocked at what he was wearing.

While trying to make his escape at night from his tent, Davis was nabbed wearing his wife's overcoat and shawl.

THE POLITICAL HALL OF SHAME

SPIT FOR SPAT

At times the floor of the U.S. House of Representatives has looked more like a wrestling ring than a legislative chamber.

In 1798 Congressman Matthew Lyon of Vermont spoke against presenting President John Adams with a formal reply to the president's annual State of the Union address.

Roger Griswold, congressman from Connecticut, didn't agree with Lyon. But rather than debate the merits of Lyon's argument, Griswold launched a personal attack on his colleague. Griswold accused Lyon of having shown cowardice during the American Revolution.

Outraged by this slander, Lyon marched over to Griswold and spit right in his face and then stormed off. Griswold then asked for a House resolution to expel the "spitting Lyon" for disorderly conduct, but it failed to pass.

Nevertheless, Griswold soon got even. Two weeks after the spitting incident, the congressman waited until after the House chaplain had conducted his daily prayer. Then Griswold walked over to where Lyon was sitting and clubbed him over the head with a large yellow hickory cane. Lyon managed to fend off further strikes by grabbing a pair of fire tongs from the House fireplace.

The two then tossed aside their weapons and threw each other down to the floor, where they rolled around, snarling and clawing at each other. Meanwhile some of the other congressmen rushed over and tried to pull them apart by their legs. "What?" shouted House Speaker Jonathan Dayton. "Take a hold of a man's legs? That's no way to take a hold of him!"

But the two brawlers were finally separated. Like a brush fire that keeps reigniting, however, Griswold and Lyon kept trying to go after each other, and fellow congressmen spent the rest of the day keeping them from renewing their battle on the House floor and in the lobby.

The following day the House adopted a resolution requiring the two men to promise that "they [would] not commit any act of violence upon each other" from that day forward. Somewhat reluctantly, Griswold and Lyon took the pledge.

According to an account at the time of the wild incident, spectators in the gallery above the House floor were disappointed about the truce. Complained one person, "There is nothing to do in Congress today. There's no fighting going on."

REPRESENTATIVES CAUGHT PLAYING HOOKY

In the 1800s congressmen faced fines and even stiffer penalties if they failed to be present during a roll-call vote. At times the House refused to continue until the House clerk literally sent out a posse to round up absent congressmen.

Late one night in 1848 the Speaker of the House ordered the doors locked and sent the House clerk out on a mission to round up all the representatives who were playing hooky. Those who were dragged back to the House faced an angry Speaker, who demanded to hear their reasons for being absent without leave.

A Maryland congressman said that since he was paid per day (as was the custom back then) rather than per *night*, he felt he hadn't avoided his duties. He was promptly fined.

Also fined were a Virginian who went home because he was hungry, and a Tennessean who went home because it was past his bedtime.

Another congressman told the Speaker, "I sat in this House for ten hours and was tired, hungry, and sleepy. I believed it would be a night of speech making and not of business. And, as I have generally been an attentive listener to speeches, I concluded I had done my share of that part of legislative duty." Accordingly, he said, he had left the House at 10 P.M. The Speaker fined him too.

While the roundup was taking place, several absent congressmen who heard that the clerk was looking for them managed to sneak back into the House even though the doors were locked. An Alabama representative slipped in through a window behind the Speaker's chair. Another congressman risked life and limb by sliding down one of the marble pillars from the gallery.

During Wild Brawl . . .

CONGRESSMAN "SCALPED" ON THE HOUSE FLOOR

As the United States crept closer to the Civil War, the House of Representatives turned into a tense, angry arena. Congressmen shook fists at each other, shouted insults, and even whipped out pistols and knives to make their point. On several occasions major brawls broke out.

It was not a fun place. But one night a free-for-all on the House floor ended with all the combatants laughing.

It happened in 1858, when the House was debating the admission of Kansas to the Union. Laurence Keitt, a fiery congressman from South Carolina, insulted Pennsylvania's Galusha Grow, who shot back, "No slave driver shall crack his whip over me!"

The two charged each other, and within seconds their friends joined in. More than a dozen congressmen were kicking, beating, punching, and wrestling on the floor.

The Speaker of the House and the sergeant-at-arms tried in vain to stop the fighting. The battle raged on until one congressman grabbed another by the hair and yanked. To his surprise he pulled a wig off his opponent's head. "Hooray, boys!" shouted the congressman. "I've got his scalp!"

Everyone started laughing, and the fighting quickly came to a happy end—happy, that is, for everyone except the man who lost his wig.

HAVE YOU LOOKED IN THE MIRROR LATELY?

Abraham Lincoln and Stephen Douglas engaged in fierce debates during their race for U.S. senator of Illinois in 1858.

One day Douglas accused Lincoln of being two-faced. Lincoln cleverly blunted the verbal attack by responding, "I leave it to my audience. If I had another face, do you think I would wear this one?"

AN APPLE A DAY
KEEPS THE HECKLERS AWAY

During his run for Congress in 1866, candidate Benjamin Butler of Massachusetts was invited to speak at a huge political rally in New York City.

To his surprise he encountered a great deal of hostility. The crowd greeted him with boos, catcalls, and hisses. Suddenly an apple flew through the air and hit him in the head.

People laughed, but they quieted down quickly when Butler pulled out a knife. The crowd grew silent, wondering if the candidate planned to attack the hecklers. Instead Butler calmly leaned down,

picked up the apple, and peeled it. Then he began eating it. "Not a bad apple at that," he announced with a smile. When he finished munching on his apple, he continued his speech—and no one heckled him.

WELL, AT LEAST HE WON'T CAST A WRONG VOTE

Pennsylvania voters elected a dead man to Congress!

In 1868 they chose to be represented in the House by Thaddeus Stevens—even though he had been dead for more than 2 ½ months.

Stevens was a fiery Republican leader in Congress who opposed slavery and the South's attempt at seceding from the Union. Stevens died in office on August 11, 1868, at the age of 76. His body lay in state in the Capitol rotunda, where 6,000 people came to pay their final respects. A week later 15,000 turned out for his funeral in Lancaster, Pennsylvania.

Soon after his burial the Lancaster County Republican Party tried to figure out who to run as a candidate for Stevens' seat in the upcoming elections. They decided on none other than the late congressman himself. As a party spokesman explained, it was a "fitting tribute to the memory of our most able and distinguished champion of freedom and justice."

The Democrats scoffed at the Republicans for running a "corpse for Congress." The voters of Lancaster County thought otherwise. They elected Stevens anyway.

Later, in a special election, another man was voted in to fill Thaddeus Stevens' seat.

THE STILLAGUAMISH, THE SNOQUALMIE, THE . . . OH, FORGET IT

In 1885 the House of Representatives was considering a bill designed to help various rivers and harbors.

Among the rivers mentioned in the bill were the hard-to-pronounce Stillaguamish, Nooksack, Snohomish, and Snoqualmie in Washington Territory. After going over the bill, Michigan congressman Byron Cutcheon offered this amendment (which was ultimately defeated): ". . . That at least one thousand dollars of the money hereby appropriated shall be used in straightening out the names of said rivers."

PENNIES FROM SOL

New York Congressman Sol Bloom had a big heart, and he demonstrated it during the bleak Great Depression years in the 1930s.

Bloom would walk up the steps of the U.S. Capitol every morning and quietly drop pennies, nickels, and dimes along the way. When asked why he did it, Bloom replied, "Let the little children find them when they come to see the Capitol. In this depression, someone has to show them that good things can happen."

AND THEY TALKED ON AND ON AND ON . . .

In order to defeat a bill, a senator in strong

physical shape can attempt a filibuster—a speech that drags on for hours and hours and thereby delays or prevents a legislative vote on a measure.

In 1908 Robert La Follette of Wisconsin set the Senate record by speaking for an exhausting 18 hours and 13 minutes against a currency bill.

In 1935 Senator Huey Long of Louisiana began a filibuster that he vowed would break La Follette's record. Long started talking against a New Deal bill at 12:30 P.M. Then he read aloud the entire U.S. Constitution and filled out his speech with such unrelated matters as cooking recipes and humorless anecdotes. Finally, at 4 A.M. the following day, after speaking for 15 ½ hours, Long dropped into his seat from physical exhaustion.

Eighteen years later, in 1953, Senator Wayne Morse of Oregon filibustered against an oil bill. Morse set a new Senate record by speaking for a fatiguing 22 hours and 26 minutes.

The new mark lasted only four years. In 1957 Strom Thurmond of South Carolina became the filibuster champion by rambling on for an incredible 24 hours and 18 minutes in his fight against a civil-rights bill.

Another South Carolina senator, Olin Johnston, told reporters he had a whopping 400-page speech ready to deliver that would surpass Morse's and Thurmond's filibusters combined. But Johnston lasted only a paltry 90 minutes.

His excuse? "My feet got tired, and so I quit."

ODD ODDS AND ENDS

WANT A WIFE? IT WILL COST YOU A BUNDLE—OF TOBACCO

In 1619 Jamestown, Virginia, was populated mostly by men, and they were getting sick and tired of looking at each other. They wanted female companionship.

To the colonists' joy the Virginia Company sent 90 well-chaperoned single women from England to the New World. The women came of their own free will, but not for free. Each man who wound up marrying one of the young women had to pay the company 120 pounds of tobacco to cover the cost of her passage.

What many men didn't know until later was that most of the women had been convicts in England. But the men were so lonely they didn't care.

NOW YOU HAVE IT, NOW YOU DON'T

The man who financed the American Revolution was proud of having helped bring about the birth of a new nation. So how did the new country repay him? By tossing him in debtor's prison!

Robert Morris of Philadelphia was once the richest man in America. He had cornered the tobacco market and controlled a vast financial empire in land, banking, and shipping. At his wealthiest, Morris managed to finance the American Revolution on his personal credit. But he lost everything when the Bank of England failed in 1797, ruining Morris' credit and his shipping interests.

Morris had speculated heavily in Western real estate. Faced with enormous debt that he couldn't pay, Morris was ordered to debtor's prison, which is where you were sent if you couldn't cover your bills. Morris refused to go to prison and held out for months in his locked mansion. But eventually he ended up at the Prune Street Jail.

One of his friends who visited him in prison was George Washington, but even the former president didn't have enough clout to spring Morris from behind bars. It took an act of Congress to do that, the Bankruptcy Act of 1800.

FRANKLIN'S TURKEY OF AN IDEA

If Benjamin Franklin had had his way, the bald eagle would not be America's great national symbol.

In 1782 Congress was trying to select a symbol for the Great Seal of the United States. Several birds were considered before the eagle was chosen. But Franklin disagreed with the decision.

In a letter to his daughter he expressed the wish

that the bald eagle had not been chosen as the representative of our country. His reasons? The bald eagle, Franklin wrote, "is a bird of bad moral character" and "does not get his living honestly." Franklin accused the eagle of liking to perch "on a dead tree, where, too lazy to fish for himself, he watches the labor of the fishing hawk" and then steals the bird's catch.

What was Franklin's choice for the symbol of America? None other than the turkey!

UMBRELLAS CREATE A STORM OF CONTROVERSY

No one thinks twice about seeing someone using an umbrella in the rain.

But back in the 1770s, when umbrellas were introduced to America, colonists mocked them. No self-respecting person would be caught dead with one. Newspapers described umbrellas as ridiculous things used by sissies.

A Philadelphia physician, however, defended the umbrella. He claimed that it could benefit health by preventing epilepsy, shading sore eyes, thwarting fevers, and curing dizziness. In fact, other than providing shade and cover, umbrellas did none of those things.

Despite its bad image, the umbrella began to gain favor with Americans—especially in areas hit hardest by rain.

FAMED NATURE LOVER
STARTS FOREST FIRE

Famed nature lover Henry David Thoreau—author of the classic *Walden, or Life in the Woods*—carelessly started a forest fire.

In 1844 Thoreau, who was then 26 years old, was with a friend camping on the banks of the Sudbury River in Massachusetts. They lit a fire in a tree stump to cook fish they had caught. Unfortunately the wind kicked up and carried ashes to nearby brush. By the time the fire was put out, more than 300 acres of forest had burned.

MAYBE WE SHOULD CALL HIM
JOHNNY APPLEWEED

Johnny Appleseed spread more than seeds for

apple trees in the Midwest. He also spread weeds.

Appleseed, whose real name was John Chapman, was a nurseryman from Massachusetts. In 1800 the 26-year-old took his sack of apple seeds to Pennsylvania and Ohio and sowed them along roadways and rivers and in forest clearings. Wearing a burlap coffee sack for a shirt and a tin mush pan for a hat, the barefoot eccentric became well known to settlers throughout the region.

Appleseed was a great believer in the power of plants as medicines, and he encouraged their use. Back then people thought that a plant called the dog fennel relieved fever. So, with the best of intentions, Appleseed scattered dog fennel seeds throughout Ohio and Indiana.

The problem was that dog fennel, a foul-smelling weed, spreads fast and grows to heights of up to 15 feet. Today the weed is regarded as a nuisance by farmers who find it around their barns and in their pastureland. Some farmers now call dog fennel "Johnnyweed."

LEAVE THE DRIVING TO SOMEONE ELSE

William Phelps Eno was responsible for modern traffic regulations—even though he never learned how to drive!

Eno, known as the father of traffic safety, originated stop signs, one-way streets, taxi stands, pedestrian safety islands, traffic rotaries, and the first manual of police traffic regulations.

Although he grew up in New York City in the 1800s before the invention of the automobile, Eno saw plenty of traffic jams. Horse-drawn wagons and buggies could tie up traffic for blocks because there were no rules of the road.

Fed up with the transportation chaos in the city, Eno published an article in 1900 titled "Reform in Our Street Traffic Urgently Needed." It instantly established his reputation as a traffic-safety engineer. Soon he was coming up with all sorts of ideas to improve the flow of traffic safely through the city. Before long his suggestions were put to use across the country and even in Europe.

Ironically, despite his great knowledge about traffic, Eno refused to learn to drive. A lifelong lover of horseback riding, Eno assumed that that new invention, the automobile, would not last. By the

1920s he realized he was wrong, and he ended up buying a car. But he wouldn't operate it. Instead he was driven around by a chauffeur.

New Yorkers Hide from Terror . . .

"A SHOCKING CARNIVAL OF DEATH!"

The streets of New York were nearly empty as people hid inside in fear—all because of a barefaced hoax.

At the turn of the century *New York Herald* publisher James Gordon Bennett once boasted to a group of friends that he could make the public do anything he wanted. To prove his claim, Bennett declared he could make almost every New Yorker remain indoors the very next day.

The following morning the streets of downtown New York were virtually deserted. That's because the headlines of the morning edition of the *Herald* screamed that dangerous, man-eating animals had escaped from the zoo. The headlines warned of "Terrible Scenes of Mutilation" and a "Shocking Carnival of Death!" The stories said that the killer animals were prowling Manhattan and terrorizing the city.

Of course, none of it was true. It took several hours for New Yorkers to realize they had been victimized by the publisher's irresponsible hoax.

THE MARTIANS HAVE LANDED!
THE MARTIANS HAVE LANDED!

People listening to a CBS radio broadcast on Halloween night, 1938, were terrified when they heard that Martians had landed and were invading New Jersey.

It was all part of a radio production of H. G. Wells' novel *War of the Worlds*. But of the estimated six million listeners, a million apparently believed the radio reports were true. Panic-stricken people cried and prayed and fled their homes to escape the Martians' death rays. Church services were interrupted by hysterics, traffic was snarled, and phone lines were jammed.

In the hour-long drama, produced by actor Orson Welles, dance music was interrupted by an announcer reporting gas explosions on Mars. More bulletins followed. A strange, flaming object had crashed outside Trenton, New Jersey. A humming sound was coming from the saucer-shaped vehicle. A reporter on the scene then shouted that something was wriggling out of the object. "It's as large as a bear and glistening like wet leather! . . . Eyes gleaming like a serpent, a V-shaped mouth with saliva dripping from rimless lips that seem to quiver and pulsate."

Other reports talked of poisonous black smoke, death rays, people dropping like flies, Martians landing all over the country, and the U.S. Army getting wiped out.

Despite four announcements during the show that this was pure fiction, a tidal wave of panic swept across the nation, reaching people who didn't even have the radio on. No broadcast in the history of radio had ever caused such hysteria.

At the end of the show Welles told his listeners, "If your doorbell rings and nobody is there, it was no Martian . . . It's Halloween."

Pilot Was Headed for California
"WRONG-WAY" CORRIGAN LANDS IN IRELAND

Pilot Douglas Corrigan flew into the history books in 1938—by going the wrong way.

Corrigan, who, days earlier, had set a California-to-New York speed record, wanted to fly across the Atlantic Ocean, but he was denied federal permission because of the rickety condition of his single-engine plane. So he decided to fly back to California.

He took off early in the morning in a blanket of fog that covered New York's Floyd Bennett Field. Then he made a wrong turn over Long Island. Corrigan misread his compass and didn't realize his mistake until he came out of the fog 24 hours later. He found himself over the country of Ireland.

"I intended to fly to California," he told the press, "but I got mixed up in the clouds and must have flown the wrong way."

From then on Corrigan was known as "Wrong-way."

THE MAIL POOCH

The U.S. Postal Service's most unusual mailman wasn't a man at all. He was Dorsey, a Border collie.

In 1883 Dorsey, a stray, was taken in by Jim Stacy, the local postmaster in Calico, California. When Stacy delivered the mail on foot, his new pet tagged along behind him.

One day Stacy fell ill and was unable to deliver the mail. But, knowing how intelligent his dog was, Stacy decided that Dorsey could fill in for him. The postmaster fashioned a crude harness with double saddlebags for Dorsey. After filling the pouches with mail, Stacy sent his dog off to East Calico with a note tied to the collar. The letter asked that people take their mail out and put any outgoing mail into the saddlebags. Dorsey successfully completed his mail round.

Once Stacy recovered, he gave the dog a special route of his own. From 1883 to 1886 Dorsey carried mail between Calico and nearby Brunswick.

Sent by Parcel Post for 53 Cents . . .
GIRL SHIPPED TO HER GRANDMOTHER— IN THE MAIL!

To save money, the parents of four-year-old May Pierstorff decided not to send the girl to her grandmother's by train. Instead of buying a train ticket, they mailed her by parcel post!

In 1914 the Pierstorffs wanted May to see her grandmother. When they realized it would cost several dollars for their daughter to travel the 100 miles from their home in Lewiston, Idaho, to Grangeville, Idaho, they thought of a less expensive way.

They took their 48-pound child to the post office to mail her. The postmaster looked up the rules and regulations for sending such a package and discovered that May fit the weight requirements.

Although it was illegal to mail most live animals, baby chicks were allowed. So the postmaster called May a baby chick, collected 53 cents in postage from her parents, and glued the stamps on the child's coat.

May was taken to the train depot and put into the mail car, where the baggage man watched over her. On her arrival in Grangeville, May was transported to the post office, where the postman took the girl to her grandmother.

Banking by Mail . . .
POST OFFICE DELIVERS ENTIRE BANK— BRICK BY BRICK

The post office once delivered 80,000 individual bricks through the mail so that a builder could construct a bank.

In 1916 contractor W. H. Coltharp promised the citizens of Vernal, Utah, that he would put up a classy building for the town's new bank. Ordinary red bricks were available locally, but he wanted to use fancy bricks that were made in Salt Lake City 150 miles away.

Because no roads linked the two cities, the cost of commercially shipping the bricks by rail or horse-drawn wagon was four times higher than the cost of the bricks themselves.

But then Coltharp had a brainstorm. He went to the post office and asked about the rates. The price for mailing the bricks by parcel post was half what he had been quoted from other shippers. The only

catch was that no package could weigh more than 50 pounds. So Coltharp ordered 40 tons of bricks to be mailed in 1,600 individually wrapped packages, each weighing 50 pounds. The bricks then arrived by train, a ton at a time.

The brick mailings created such controversy that U.S. postal regulations were rewritten so that one person could receive no more than 200 pounds of mail per day. "It's not the intention of the Post Office Department that buildings should be shipped through the mail," declared then-U.S. Postmaster General A. S. Burleson.

Today the "bank by mail" is still standing in Vernal, Utah.